IN MY WILDEST DREAMS

Sue Freeman

Dedications

Thanks to Cousin Neil for the opportunity and the gift of a lifetime (bragging rights, that is).

Thank you MAO, Jeanne, and Kate for your kind and gentle editing tips.

To my dad and Neil, thanks for your encouragement when I was ready to give up on publishing.

Thanks to my little band of cheerleaders: Margaret, Sandy, Carol, Moira and my ever lovin' BFF Cathy.

CONTENTS

FOREWORD 4

BEFORE 5

EN ROUTE 29

ARRIVAL... 35

THE HIKE UP 41

THE HIKE DOWN.. 73

HELLZ YEAH FINAL DAY'S HIKE 79

CELEBRATION 85

HOME SWEET HOME 91

PERSONAL PICKS & RECOMMENDATIONS.......... 95

SPECIAL MENTIONS... 101

FOREWORD

What happens when a 5'1" and shrinking, menopausal Mississippi Gulf Coast Jewish homemaker is offered the adventure of a lifetime to climb Mt. Kilimanjaro, Africa's highest peak, with only six weeks notice?

TOTAL FREAK OUT INDEED!

After gaining consciousness, I began to scour the internet for a woman's perspective on the experience, only to find absolutely zero, zilch, nada. Because there was no female perspective on the subject, I was inspired to keep this journal account from beginning to end, encouraged by Phil Gray's book titled *Mt. Kilimanjaro via the Marangu Route: 'Tourist Route' My Ass,* written upon his survival, er, return. Similarly, I found the humorous "ups and downs" of the hike just too ridiculous to keep it all to myself.

Hope y'all enjoy!

BEFORE

My husband, Mac, is in Tallahassee on business and I am so looking forward to having the bed all to myself to read with the light ON as long as I want. The laundry is almost finished. Removing the towels from the dryer, I nuzzle into their warmth for some much needed soothing. Our beloved yellow tabby, AmberJack, is in final stages of renal/kidney failure. My other nagging worry is our financial status or rather the lack of. Since Hurricane Katrina we have been chipping away at debt left in her wake, yet we find ourselves still floundering underwater. My new part-time job as a greeting card merchandiser helps somewhat, but my stomach is still in knots despite *Downy* fresh warmth of the towels. (I swear the rest of this book is not as depressing as that first paragraph).

The phone rings loudly and I practically jump out of my skin. Who could be calling this late? Has one of my elderly parents "fallen and they can't get up...." or worse? Is Mac in jail for DUI? Caller ID says *Potomac, MD,* so it must be Cousin Neil. Six weeks apart in age, we've shared a special bond all of our lives despite miles between his home in Maryland and mine in Alabama (now Mississippi). It's been a while since I last spoke with Neil, but it's still an unusually late hour for him to call.

Neil: *What are you doin'?*

Sue: *Laundry (yawn), what about you? How's training going for your Kilimanjaro expedition?"*

Neil: *Well, as a matter of fact ...... a guy in our group cancelled and you're the only one I know in good enough shape to do it on short notice.*

Sue: *NO WAY! You're kidding, right?!*

Neil: *No, I'm not kidding and I really want you to go. Martha Stewart even did it! So did Ann Curry, but she*

—

7

didn't make it all the way due to an altitude problem or something.

Sue: *Wow, what a fantastic opportunity! But to be honest, I can't afford expenses for this kind of trip – the clothes, the gear and all.*

Neil: *Don't worry about that part. It's all on me. Happy Birthday! Go shopping. Anyway, I'm emailing you the details right away. Check it out and I'll call you tomorrow. You can tell me then yes or no, but I really,* **REALLY** *want you to go!*

Sue: *No matter if I can go or not, your invitation alone is an honor in itself. I love you just for inviting me!*

I begin hopping around the house like a crazy energizer bunny while my heart is pounding out its own rock solo. I want to tell Mac so badly, but it's late. I text him instead: OMG, OMG, OMG!!!! Neil called tonight inviting me to join him on the Kilimanjaro trip in June (his treat)! A member of the group cancelled & I was his 1st choice! Can u believe this?! Should I wait until morning to open Neil's email with the trip details? No, I can't resist. Counting three …two … one … Click. Open Sesame:

Epic Kilimanjaro
By EPIC PRIVATE JOURNEYS
A Private Journey for Party of six
21 to 29 June 2009

A daunting amount of information unfolds. A recommended training regimen is included (*but no regimen for my twenty feet above sea level*), their contact info (*proof to my family I'm not running away with the UPS man*), Tanzanian Visa address (*home of the Tanzanian Devil?*), lodging description

—

8

complete with pictures (*shoulders relax*), geographical and historical data (I w*onder if climbing next to the equator helps with balance?*), typical weather conditions are warm, cool and frigid (*basically every season*), sample itinerary (*too chicken to read now*), safety and medical information (*shoulders tighten back*), effects of altitude (*my eyes bulge*). Last, but certainly not least, is an incredibly long, intimidating supply and gear list and more. To the bathroom I run, (*runner up for this book's title*) thanks to a nervous stomach.

It's late now. I have an early wake-up tomorrow for work and I need sleep. Yeah, like that's gonna happen. *Please, please let me find Mac's Ambien stash!* After much bathroom and toiletry kit rummaging, I find some, along with $4.78 in change.

Thanks to a good night's rest (compliments of the tiny white pill), I'm ready to get on with my full day. PIYO (Pilates- yoga) class is first up for core strengthening. The last thing I need now is back trouble. With adrenalin pulsating, I bounce through the studio door. My classmates sense my nervous energy, so I spill the beans on my upcoming adventure. Some react with open-mouth stares and a loss for words, as if I'd announced I was going half way across the world to hike, not bathe for five days, and eat white bread. Others come lunging with full embraces shouting *"You go girl!"* How I love these yoga goddesses! My regular walking buds tease, *"Can't wait to see you walking the bridge in your hiking boots. And you think your sock tan line is bad now!"*

After class, greeting card merchandising, and preparing dinner, I make time to peruse EPIC's email attachment again. The overview of Africa and Kilimanjaro is exciting. The training agenda is over-the-top, not to mention I am already six months behind the rest of the group. SHIT SHIT SHIT! This makes fall's Susan G. Komen 3-Day Breast Cancer Walk seem like a stroll in the park! And the packing list is insanely overwhelming:

—
9

CLOTHING

2 pair of shorts.
NO WAY! I outlawed shorts three years ago!

2 pairs of lightweight trousers.
Now you're talking'!

Wide brim hat for shade against the sun.
War Eagle or Longhorn caps?

Two t-shirts, one collared shirt.
White or blue?

Water/windproof trousers & hooded anorak, preferably with a Gore-Tex shell to cope with wind/rain at differing temperatures.
We're going to get wet?

Three warm upper body layers (synthetic or woolen) that can fit comfortably over each other.
Sounds like a fun parlor game!

Waterproof gloves or mittens; thin under-gloves.
My fingers are numbing already.

Balaclava.
We bring our own dessert?

One pair of warm fleece-type trousers.
You had me at "warm."

Waterproof, breathable gaiters.
GAITERS .... SERIOUSLY, a bayou joke at my expense?!

Broken-in hiking boots and spare laces.
Spare laces, in case we need to make a tourniquet? And my boots should be broken in by now? I have yet to click a boots ORDER button.

2 pairs of thermal underwear, lighter pair to wear as inner set, heavier pair for extra warmth.
Perhaps I should reconsider. Should someone like me with Raynaud's Disease hike in frigid conditions? At fifty degrees or below, my fingers and toes lose circulation. First they become numb and then morph into a sickly shade of dead.

Thick socks, 6 pairs woolen or synthetic.
Hope they are available in XXX thick.

EQUIPMENT
Camelbak hiking backpack.
Finally, an item I have!
Water bottle – 2 litre, wide mouth.
As in 2- liter bottles? Man, that's some heavy totin'!
Insulated tube cover.
For lip balm?
Headlamp
Are we mining too?!
Spare torch batteries/bulb.
African torches run on batteries?

OPTIONAL EQUIPMENT
Water purification tablets (the water provided en route is a combination of bottled mineral water and mountain stream water, which is double-pumped and purified).
Imodium reminder.
Walking pole.
I take it no relation to a stripping pole.
Water flavoring (to mask the taste resulting from purification methods).
Why not vodka? Solve two problems at once.
Gel-activated hand/footwarmers.
Hopefully cheaper by the dozen!
High-energy bars for the final ascent, especially as appetite can be suppressed by high altitude.
Ooooooh – can we bottle that?

I generally don't spend much on clothes unless a special occasion arises. We live modestly here on the Mississippi Gulf Coast. Moreover after losing so many *things* to Hurricane Katrina, I've gained a renewed appreciation for the non-material, family, friends, and pets. I begin to check online for hiking outfitter websites. Wow, this stuff sure don't come cheap! It's not even my money I'm about to spend, and it's making me physically sick. But order I must, so I stab at a few sites such as Altrec.com, BackCountry.com, and before I get to Rei.com, I am sprinting to the bathroom.

My youngest daughter, Jillian, walks into the kitchen peering at my virtual shopping bag and shouts, *"Mom, you should've married Neil!"* I crack up and admit that I'd genuinely felt the same way when we were little. Not because of his family wealth, but because I simply LOVED being around his adorable and fun-loving spirit. Even at age fifty-five, a CEO and board member of several well-known and respected institutions, he still makes me giggle like time has stood still. I bet he can still recite the theme songs to "Gilligan's Island," "The Beverly Hillbillies," and "The Addams Family."

Now what was it he mentioned about Martha Stewart and Ann Curry? To research these two adventuresses and their experiences climbing Mt. Kilimanjaro, I Google *Martha Stewart Kilimanjaro* only to find one entry entailing how she met the current president of her company on the hike. All of the other links highlight various stories of people puking their way up the mountain due to altitude sickness. O great!! Ann Curry's story was worse. She never made it to the summit due to cerebral edema. My palms begin to sweat, still surfing, scouring the Net. *Oy vey*, here it is:

"Climbing Mt. Kilimanjaro is no small feat; a very healthy guy in his 40's from my town died while climbing it not long ago and another guy suffered life threatening altitude sickness a few 100 yards from the summit."

YIKES! What have I gotten myself into?! Back to the bathroom I run. Surely, there must be other women's blogs or accounts of "Kili" experiences for me to gain a better perspective. I search again, only to come up with basic statistics ... freezing cold temps, stomach and altitude issues, *yadda yadda yadda*. There is also a recurrent theme on fundraiser treks as well as an article about *Comic Relief* sponsoring celebs to hike for charity. Now I feel selfish and petty in wanting to learn about simple hygiene at camp and the real *scoop* on the potty situation. Does one carry a personal poop bag and pooper scooper like my dog lover friends? Is there going to be an orientation on safe shrubbery wipes? For once I am content with my menopausal age, no worries over cycle timing and that ensuing paraphernalia. Enough! This is starting to stress me out. Just step away from the computer!

Between Kili on the brain, my miserably sick kitty, and daughter Kate's out of state summer tuition bill looming, I am not sleeping or eating well. At least a Mother's Day trip to Birmingham, Alabama is coming up and I can finally get a handle on the long supply list at a *Mountain Outfitters* store. My brain rudely interrupts, *"Passport... Where is it?!"* Not in the kitchen desk or bedroom drawers, perhaps upstairs in one of the kids' desks. Why? Why not? House elves work in mysterious ways. Staying calm climbing the stairs, I know I've seen it somewhere. I pray that when I find it, it hasn't expired. I climb back downstairs (hey, this can count for a climbing workout). Open a drawer. YES, I found it!! Other than cringing at its rippled pages ala Katrina, I am relieved to see the expiration date is well within range. *Whew*!

The Tanzania Consulate's website is easy to access. I can't believe I sit here about to fill out a visa application for Tanzania, Africa! So exciting, but I begin to freak out after reading the travel advice section. You'd think we were going to a third-world country. Oh yeah, we are. This is what appears as the site opens:

Malaria is a serious concern in Tanzania. *WHAT??!* **Also certain inoculations are recommended for travel to Africa. Please consult your General Practitioner or nearest Traveler's Medical Centre for advice. As a general guideline you will need a combination of the following:**
Hepatitis A and B ... *Can't remember*
Meningococcal Meningitis ... *Can't remember*

13

Polio … *Can't remember*
Typhoid … *Can't remember*
Cholera … *Can't remember*
Tetanus … *Can't remember*
Yellow Fever - this is now mandatory in order to gain entry to Tanzania. You will be required to present your inoculation certificate upon arrival.
I remember! Definitely never had!

I can't help but wonder about the other members in our hiking group. My cousin mentioned there would be three women and three men, but no other details. Isn't it natural to be curious who will be seeing you at your worst for six days, seven nights?! Are they experienced climbers? Are they jocks? Are they aged thirty, forty, or fiftyish? On my next phone chat with Neil, I get the courage to ask about our fellow travelers.

Sue: *Neil, are the others in the group our age, younger, or older?*

Neil: *Ages thirty-five to fifty.*

Sue: *So we'll be the old farts of the group, huh? Am I the only mountain climbing virgin on this expedition?*

Neil: *We're all virgins!*

After our chat, I return to the Internet to complete gear purchases. I have less than a month to return items that may not fit. Gotta love Zappos.com and Shoes.com for free shipping both ways! Before I pull up the dreaded list, I check my email for new notes from Neil or the trip organizers. One is from Neil and another is a group email from Brad himself:

Hi All,
Hope this finds you all well and that your

14

preparations for Kili are coming on. Just a month to d-day. I am off on the 9th of June for a safari to trek and paddle the Zambezi prior to the climb.

What is this guy – a Tarzan wannabe?

I want to take this opportunity to see where each of you are at with the following:

Geez Louise ...MORE lists?!

Tanzania visa requirements include:

1. A complete visa application form.

Can do.

2. Valid Passport

Withered and waterlogged, but still valid.

3. Two recent passport photographs.

Wonder if photo must match tired- ass face after flying umpteen hours?

4. A sufficiently stamped self-addressed envelope for return of passport by secure mail.

The "Forever" stamp isn't good enough?

5. Visa fees: U.S. visa fee is $100 for both six months. Single and twelve-month multiple entry.

No discount for six days?

6. Provide proof of travel plans to and from Tanzania.

Did Cicero send a warning message to Africa?
"Both fish and guests stink after three days."

7. Provide proof of having sufficient funds to maintain the applicant while in Tanzania - via bank statements, employer letter, or pay stubs.

What ....having a rich cousin isn't enough?!

In addition:

1. Training - by now you should be doing a fair amount of long pack-walks (as per the suggested training program). **Your boots should be by now worn in and not causing any discomfort.**

ROFLMAO (Rolling On the Floor, Laughing My Ass Off)

2. Travel insurance - having travel cover is mandatory for the climb, for medical reasons in **addition to cancellation, loss of luggage etc.**

If my luggage is lost, I will take it as a sign from G-d.

———

3. Medical - Yellow Fever shot is mandatory. Also, if you wish to take Diamox (altitude medication) whilst on the mountain please ensure you trial it prior to embarkation.
Hoping side effects are superpowers!!

Neil
Received Brad's note this morning & wondering when you arranged my flights, was insurance added for lost baggage, medical, etc? Are U climbing in CO this weekend? If so, have fun. Add 100 lbs for training in case u wind up having to carry my ass. Love, Sue

Sue,
Not a big insurance guy, so don't lose anything, don't get sick and show up!!! On way to CO. Hopefully will get a hike or two in ... XO Neil
(Neil, a mountain climbing virgin, my ass!!)

After days of searching fruitlessly online for more Kili blogs, I have an epiphany to check video rental websites for anything on Kilimanjaro. To my delight, I come across a documentary, *"Kilimanjaro,The Roof of Africa!"* In the film, there are climbers of various ages, ranging in ages from twelve to seventy-five. I definitely get a feel for the beauty, the arduous climbing involved, and the unpredictable effects of altitude from person to person. Life is certainly full of surprises. I've always dreamt of going to Africa, but on a photo safari, not so much climbing to this "Roof of Africa!" What they don't show are the climbing potty breaks or the middle of the night *interruptions*. Am I obsessed? U betcha! My mom told me soon after I became aware of *Ladies Rooms*, she worried I might have a bladder problem. Every restaurant we went to, I'd make a beeline for the facilities. I confess it wasn't so much the need to *go*, it was more the curiosity factor. I just wanted to see the decor, having been impressed at an early age with a few fancy-schmancy ones complete with sofas, ornate vanities and such. You might say they were my

---

secret gardens, so feminine, perfumed and exotic. Best of all, they were off limits to my two older brothers. Naturally I had my share of disappointments too, which returns my thoughts to the so far, unmentionable mountain bathroom facilities. I just can't picture the refined Martha Stewart roughing it, or rather *rock squatting,* her way up the mountain. Bet she had porters tote 2-ply Charmin, which reminds me to pack my own roll (as recommended in the guide's packing list). My not-so-secret fear is really the bathroom issue. I could very well give new meaning to LMAO (Laughing My Ass Off) … a cliff!!!

Neil calls to see how things are progressing.

Neil: *You're never going to guess what else is recommended for altitude sickness. Viagra!! And I'm not kidding. A close medical friend of ours emailed me the info. I'll send it to you.*

Sue: *(chuckling) Maybe we shouldn't share a tent now.*

Neil: *Well, at least it'll stay up!*

My list of trepidations is growing. Ok guys, let's face it. I'm fifty-five years old and no spring chicken, not to mention nearing menopause. I can only hope my hot flashes make their debut as I ascend the summit. *O Glory B to the Universe that should only happen.* Another concern of mine is pure vanity. Will I return from the climb donning a partial Fu Manchu? (Men readers, if any, you should probably skip this page. Young women take heed, while women my age you will nod your heads knowingly). There are these mysterious black or white steely chin hairs that seem to sprout within a day's time. I take vengeance upon them every night as my pre-bedtime ritual. Pluck, Pluck …. Oh pluck it. I have no problems disregarding make-up, bathing, or shaving legs for a week, but disregarding plucking? No way! Packing list amended: tweezers and hand mirror. And speaking of

---

hygiene, no showers for a week, no sloughing of dead sweaty skin cells? Man, my back is going to explode into a minefield of blackheads. Even worse, what about icky, itchy yeast infections that afflict us women when *down below* isn't properly sanitized? I can only hope *Personal Wet Cleansing Cloths* are enough to stave them off. I make a note to order additional anti-microbe panties (*Ex-Officio* brand) to be safe. Or should I just go with astronaut diapers to eliminate midnight potty hunts? On second thought, those may not have the anti-microbe feature nor would they make the green environmentally friendly list.

Neil recommends Phil Grey's book, **Kilimanjaro via the Marangu Route "Tourist Route" My Ass.** The author concurs with Kilimanjaro internet blogs about headaches that occur with most climbers due to altitude pressure on the brain. As if my brain cells weren't damaged enough from the sixties and seventies! If you see a little old lady twenty years from now with lipstick on her eyebrows (ala my eighty-two year old grandma, bless her heart, and may she rest in peace), that shall be moi. I find it interesting that everyone blames headaches on Kili's altitude, but there could be another theory, FOUR days without coffee. HELLO?! All accounts list tea as the standard hot beverage served on the climb. And we all know for us true blooded Americans, without coffee our ability to function is reduced to Zombie mode. Take care to note any photo documentation of climbers making their ascent toward the summit and observe the Frankensteinish carriage in their stilted movements. Never mind they begin summit climbs before midnight and continue well beyond dawn.

Off to my parents in Birmingham for Mother's Day weekend and a stop at *Mountain Outfitters* on the way. The manager treats me like mountain royalty, assisting with the monumental task of procuring the required gear list. While I try on countless layers, pants, jackets, hats, she scurries to the upstairs loft fetching me all kinds of gear. If they don't have an item, she quickly runs behind the front counter to search online, and emails each link to me. It is reassuring to finally get live input from a female with experience on frigid mountain climbs, and one who is very familiar with my staggering list of hiking accoutrement. I leave the shop with an overflowing bag of items, but as I begin to mark items off the list, the list seemingly grows even longer. Am I in some mountain gear Twilight Zone feature of the week? How can this be? Have I mentioned already how much I detest shopping?

When I return to the coast, there is good news and bad. The good news is my boots order arrived. Yippeekiyokayay!! The sad, bad news is that kitty AmberJack's condition has worsened. He is not eating or drinking and has red rimmed eyes and a bloody crusted mouth. I call the vet to make the dreaded appointment. The next day, I tenderly wrap him in one of my old shirts and drive to the vet's office. I tell him how much he has meant to me, to the family and thank him for his healing powers and for all the love he's given us over the past fifteen years. The vet offers time alone with him to cuddle and cry. She injects him and within ten seconds he is out, but his body still lies warm in my lap. Sigh.

I head home with a heavy heart, eager for the distraction of trying on boots. I pull them on and Damn-Blast-It, they're uncomfortable and rub harshly against my ankles, even with doubled socks! These are the Columbian Titanium Daska from Zappos.com for $139.95. My frugal attempt at purchasing cheaper hiking boots kicks my ass. At least I still have time to order a different brand. This time I'm going with the Zanbori 310 Skill GT Hiking boot for $230.00, hoping they live up to the extra cost. Looking at my list of purchases so far, I try to disregard my nervous bellyache. Maybe I should slug a vodka shooter for every item ordered to take the edge off? Hey, a new drinking game for the shopping challenged! Line up shot glasses, fill 'em up, add item to cart, salute, slam it and repeat.

A new email in from Cousin Neil:

Sue
Hope your buying stuff you can use again! Talk to
you soon;
Neil

Neil
Not much need 4 thermal undies on the Gulf Coast,
but gaiters & headlamp will definitely come in
handy if ever another hurricane!
Sue

Kate returns home for a short break from college in between spring and summer classes. She hands me a large envelope with glee in her eyes. I can feel inside is one of her original hand-crafted birthday cards and I can't wait to see what she's created. The card is embellished in an array of colorful feathers. The majestic Mt. Kilimanjaro graces its front cover and beneath is imprinted in a bold header:
There is an ancient saying in the land of KILIMANJARO.
Inside the card are the complete *Hakuna Matata* lyrics from *The Lion King* along with a special birthday message. Did you know the geographical setting of the movie is Tanzania? Such an awesome card and I am certainly not biased at all!

> *HAKUNA MATATA. WISHING YOU "HAKANA*
> *MATATA" FOR YOUR BIRTHDAY AND THE*
> *MOUNTAIN THAT AWAITS. HAPPY BIRTHDAY!!*
> *Love, Kate*

Multiple packages are beginning to arrive. I'm getting confused as to what fits, what should be packed, what to be returned. Kate ventures into my bedroom to view the hiking collection, but finds mostly various and sundry piles of mountain gear. *"Hey, Mom, your room looks like a crazy mountain expedition fire sale!"* I laugh recalling a recent breast cancer walk shared with my niece Sarah. She loves to remind me of my frequent tent confusion, *"Where is ...? I can't find...!"* Maybe that experience will benefit my African camping experience. Nah, there will probably be more lost and found episodes, not unlike my eighty-eight year old parents' re-run scenarios.

To break in my new boots, I hike the treadmill at ten percent incline level for at least two hours a day. The sweat pours off like never before. On alternate days I walk the *Ocean Springs/Biloxi Bridge*, quite literally working my butt off and in-between attend Pilates/yoga classes. I started out weighing in at 103 pounds, and after a week or so, am down to 98. Oprah, I dare you to try this weight loss regimen! My tightest britches are so loose, they slide down my hips with every stoop. Yep, just call me *"Sue the Plumber."* But here's the rub. At 98 pounds soaking wet, why does unsightly cellulite still linger on my thighs? As much as I exercise, eat healthy (a vegetarian for the past three yrs), and seldom consume alcohol, it just ain't right, I tell ya. Light bulb moment! Scientists should consider studying cellulite as a renewable source of energy. Think of all of the women who would gladly donate. Dimpled buttocks and thighs would become the new symbol of sustainability. Imagine the possibilities, providing perhaps even a new fuel resource! What to call it .... *Gasullite, FlaburFuel, Cheesoline?*

Ocean Springs/Biloxi Bridge

In-between training times, I hunt down yellow fever serum which seems like a search for the Holy Grail. Well, that's how it seems in South Mississippi. The conversation below is a sample of my experience with the county's health clinic:

> Me: *Good Afternoon. Can you tell me if the clinic has gotten in yellow fever serum yet?*

> Evil Clinic Nurse: *Sorry, we're out. We got in only five doses and they were all gone by noon.*

> Me: *Can someone call me when another shipment arrives?*

> Evil Nurse: *NO, that is NOT allowed! And don't be asking me 'bout no crack either!* (Did she really say this? No, but her attitude did)

However, I don't panic, but proceed to post on *Facebook:* **Help Needed to Locate Yellow Fever Serum**. Within thirty minutes postings pop up. A special thanks to niece Sarah for suggesting I contact the CDC in Atlanta. A location is found in Mobile, AL after going to the CDC website where it lists yellow fever vaccine clinics within any given area. After weeks of serum searching, I have advice for those traveling to countries that require vaccines. Check if your area has a *Passport Health*. It is pricey, but the clinics provide info on all immunizations needed and can also write scripts for *Diamox, Ambien*, or whatever medications your trip may require. Over the weekend I test *Diamox*, an altitude medication, to make sure there is no allergic reaction. To my tremendous relief, there is none. Unfortunately, no super-powers either.

    I am down to a week's countdown. According to my flight schedule, I'll have a whopping sum of twenty-two airport layover hours. For $90.00, I can purchase a thirty-day Sky Club membership (with birthday cash) which would offer more comfort, free snacks and beverages. If only I had a

---

laptop computer. Maybe I can find a rental or better yet, try to borrow from youngest daughter. Computer rental fees list around $115.00 a month, not including shipping and insurance. Let's think about this. I need a laptop, and Jillian needs cash. I see her eyeing pages in a new clothing catalog. Perfect timing! I approach calmly and casually. I summon my best used car salesman persona, *"Jill, I have an offer for you to consider. I'll trade you cash in return for renting your laptop for two weeks, and you can use my desktop while I'm away."* Her eyes light up with cartoon dollar signs. I walk away to the treadmill, keeping fingers crossed she'll take the deal. With most teens, this would be a done deal. But Jillian is the unpredictable type, born under the sign of Aquarius, whose reactions are never the norm. Two hours later we have a deal, and I feel as if I've just cut a trade deal with North Korea.

Tomorrow my son will return a borrowed large duffel bag. There will be no more excuses to delay sorting and packing. What to pack to check through at the airport (perhaps never to see again), and what to secure in my carry-on and backpack? Sheesh. I just about need to take a Valium or a thirty minute meditation session to pack for a simple weekender to Birmingham. At least for this trip, there's no need to coordinate accessories such as earrings, purses, etc. Next question is whether to leave or wear my engagement and wedding rings. Ann Curry's Kili experience certainly freaked me out. One account rumored her bands almost had to be cut off due to swelling from edema. My bands have only been removed for cleaning, occasional manicures, three C-sections, and one MRI scan on my lower back. Oh geez, now I'm reminded of back issues. Not sure I even want to go there, suffice it to say I have a lower back issue due to a combination of scoliosis and a really lousy chiropractor. For this expedition, I'm just gonna put a LOT of faith in ibuprofen and pray it doesn't let me down.

"MOM, THE MAILMAN'S AT THE DOOR!" It must be the duffel bag from *Epic Private Journeys*. The package is post-

marked *Australia,* Epic's office headquarters. Wow, is it heavy! Attached inside the large box appears to be sea foam colored padded filler, but it isn't. It's a *North Face* polar fleece jacket embossed with **Epic Private Journeys** in my size and very classy, even if not my color. I know this sounds petty ('cause it is). From my childhood dental visits, I developed an aversion to pastel greens, flash-backs of the dental hygienist's uniform. What the heck, it's a gift. I'll get over it. Under the jacket there is a leather embossed itinerary/passport/ticket holder along with a complete map of Mt. Kilimanjaro, illustrating every route imaginable in considerable detail. I am more excited, nervous and scared than ever now ... which sends me running once again back to the loo.

Three days to go! My first packing attempt has begun with great trepidation. My travel pants seem to be lacking a travel shirt. Did I mention how much I detest shopping?! Yet here I go, back to Gulfport in search of travel wear. Ugh. On the upside, it's a relief to have a diversion from packing. But when I return from yet another shopping trip, a nervous breakdown ensues. The phone is ringing off the hook. There are work issues, my daughter's work issues, and now the insulating camelback's neoprene sleeve (to prevent freezing) doesn't fit the tubing.

Two days to go and my work issues are under control, daughter's issues have chilled, and my Georgia Tech grad husband adroitly solved the tube insulation dilemma with some delightfully chic duct tape. There will absolutely be NO confusion which backpack belongs to the gal from Mississippi. I stop and reflect on Mac's fantastic attitude towards this trip. He's genuinely excited for me and has been enthused from the get-go. Then my soap opera infected mind kicks in. What if he's really having an affair and is really secretly tickled that I will be out of his hair (ha, he's bald) for two weeks? What if he's taken out a large insurance policy on me and paid some-one to nudge me off a cliff?!

Countdown is on. One day to go before departure. Early morning walk on the *Biloxi-Ocean Springs Bridge*, then to shower. I weigh just out of curiosity, what with all the training and nervous tummy episodes. Holy Moly! Now wondering if I should've beefed up over the past couple of weeks before this strenuous climb? Suddenly I have a craving for a thick almond butter schmear on pita toast. Seriously y'all, if I return eight pounds lighter as did author Phil Gray of *"Kili - Tourist Route My Ass,"* it's gonna be Waffle House, come to mama as soon as I get back to the coast.

As I run my last laundry load of socks for the trip, I notice the outdoor thermometer registering at a whopping 107 degrees. Three days from now in a mountain chill, my body will surely be shouting *WTF!*

Aight, I am finally not only packed, but I have checked and double checked my packing list. I am calm, cool and chillaxed. Martha Stewart would be so proud, yet annoyed at me for preparing a Rachel Ray recipe for dinner. It has a comforting, yet nutritious pre-travel meal appeal (and too delicious not to share) >>>>>>>>>>>>>>>>>>>>>>>>>>>>>

Swiss Chard and White Bean Frittata

2 large eggs, lightly beaten
½ tsp. sea salt
¼ tsp. black pepper
7 large egg whites, lightly beaten
1 tbl. finely chopped jalapeno pepper
4 chopped pitted Kalamata olives
1 (16 oz) can navy beans, rinsed & drained
2 c. torn fresh spinach or chard
¾ c. cooked brown rice
½ c. fresh grated parmesan cheese

Place egg whites, eggs, salt & pepper in a large bowl and whisk together. Stir in jalapeno, olives and beans. Heat a small amount of olive oil in a large non-stick skillet over medium high heat. Add spinach or chard; Sauté until tender. Pour the egg mixture into pan, reduce heat to medium low. Cook 15 minutes or more until almost set. Sprinkle the parmesan cheese on top. Broil until golden brown.

After dinner, my friend texts; **Packed? Ya think you'll be able to sleep tnite?!** Wow, I hadn't even given that a moment's thought, but thanks 'cause now I am. Maybe I should've gone with a pasta dinner, something heavy and drowsy. Oh well, my plan is to convince my brain that I'm just flying to Atlanta. Worry about one stop at a time, right?

I dream of a tall, dark, and handsome man strapping me into some kind of *thrill ride*, but my legs are so short that my feet don't quite fit securely into the foot holds. He is unbothered by these particulars, but my sense of security is rattled. The next thing I know, he has bound his body to mine and before I can scream, *"THIS DOESN'T FEEL SAFE AT ALL,"* we are blasting off into a black, but starry filled night sky. The air is cool and crisp. The feeling is total exuberance. I can hear myself, "OH YES! O YES, THIS IS THE BEST EVER!" Sadly, it's over in a snap, the proverbial blink of an eye. Sigh. I ask him, *"Can we do that AGAIN?!"* The strange and beautiful blue-eyed man simply looks at me and laughs. I wake hoping the dream is an omen for my Epic Journey to the Roof of Africa… exciting, but safe.

—

EN ROUTE

The alarm sounds and I pop up from my toasty bed, hit the shower, do hair and make-up, and then pack up last minute toiletries. I remember to grab my 3-Day Breast Cancer charm necklace. The idea came to me around 2 a.m. to simply slip my rings over the chain to avoid an Ann Curry swollen finger snafu. I make a mental note to grab plastic bags for dirty clothes, but I wind up forgetting them. This necessitates a stop on the way to the airport for Quik Mart's stanky lemon *fresh* trash bag alternatives. What else have I forgotten? Oh well, whatev. It's too late now.

At Gulfport airport's self check-in kiosk, I log in with my frequent flier number. The screen displays my name and itinerary. Breathe and relax. Something unfamiliar flashes, *"Swipe your passport now."* Where? Arrows direct me to "Swipe." Nothing happens. Then again, *"Swipe your passport now!"* Is this machine yelling at me now? I swipe again, this time with all the speed and grace of a thirty year old veteran cashier. Still, there is no confirmation. I turn to look at the uniformed counter agents who seem to be doing nothing, but enjoying morning banter with each other. Summoning my best puppy dog eyes, I plead for assistance. They motion for me to bring bags and passport to the counter. Upon viewing my Katrina rippled passport, he explains the computer's inability to scan my document and deftly handles it himself. Score one point for human beings! My next slight apprehension concerns the duffel bag's weigh in. Oh please, please, be less than fifty pounds. Hurrah, my bag weighs a svelte thirty-five pounds. Onward to security. I'm relieved there isn't a long line, something to be said for small town airports. All of the security guards are beaming at me in a cocky kind of way. I detect bemusement in their eyes at the pint-sized, over-the-hill woman dressed like she has a date with Smokey the Bear or the late Steve Irwin. One wise guy officer can't resist commenting on my boots as they roll along the conveyor belt, *"Ya know, you'll have to buy a new pair of boots when you grow outta these!"* Very cute, hardy-har.

The flight to Atlanta is smooth and on time. In the International concourse, I find a currency exchange office to convert U.S. dollars to shillings. In front of me is another American buying Euros at a rate sadly higher than what was available yesterday (according to his eye rolling wife). My turn next, but only South African money is available, no shillings. They are not certain whether Amsterdam will have shillings either. Thank G-d for plastic.

Off to the departure gate and my last land potty stop for quite a while. I'm looking forward to a window seat and hoping to have a spare one adjacent. I realize that's like hoping to be upgraded to first class. International gates are so cool, the assorted accents, and the fun of guessing nationalities. OOH, I hope there's not an overly large person seated next to me. That presents such an awkward exit to bathroom situation. But the KLM gods have been kind. My seat mate is a slim thirtyish raven-haired Czech woman. We smile and nod at our mutual good seating fortune.

When my vegetarian meal is delivered, it consists of mystery ravioli covered in tomato sauce. I don't know which disturbs me more, fear of its tofu filling (I am allergic to soybeans) or the big splat of tomato sauce that just plopped onto my forty-eight hour travel safari shirt. The accompanying marinated bean salad I felt safer to leave inside its plastic encasement rather than inside my wayfaring stomach, if nothing else for the consideration of other passengers. These caterers left no flatulent bean amiss in this cocktail of potential disaster... limas, garbanzos, black beans, kidney beans, fava beans, plus chopped onions. I swear this is no exaggeration. Some KLM chef certainly has a whack sense of humor! I am happy for packing a trustworthy trail mix of cereal, almonds and raisins, which I plan to chase with a dose of *Ambien*.

Unfortunately there is no restful sleep, only contortion and discomfort. Lights pop on and I smell warm hand towels a comin'. Surely breakfast will be edible and happily, it is. There's something akin to a Spanish omelet between two

---

delicious pastry slices, to hell with whole grains. There is also fresh fruit, yogurt and a cute mini banana bread loaf. Watch out Kili, this carb loaded mama is headed your way!

The plane lands in Amsterdam at last, and the search is on for my next gate connection. As it turns out, it is located at the end of a very long moving sidewalk corridor. I spy another currency exchange counter and stop by hoping to find shillings. Negative. I make my way to the ladies room to brush teeth, apply deodorant and refresh make-up, all the while feeling as if I'm walking in my sleep, toting backpack and carry-on, achy and tired. What the hey, this makes good practice for walking red-eyed attached to a heavy pack. Maybe I should grab a snack while here, but I think better yet to check boarding times. Monitor, monitor, where art thou? Aaack, it's past boarding time! Am I in some kind of time warp or what? I hustle to my boarding gate, passing other gates filled with throngs of passengers. As I approach, there's a long ass line. *"Is this the line for the Kilimanjaro flight?"* I ask the gentleman nearby. He responds in a British accent, *"Yes, we do LOVE our queues!"* The line takes about forty minutes. Again we must remove shoes, er boots, all electronics, liquids, and so on. Security is scrutinizing my *"travel size"* contact lens solution bottle which has now become subject of their great Dutch debate. Geez, not only is it labeled *"travel-size,"* but *planely* displays a *Security for Dummies* graphic of a jet plane! At last they announce their judgment call, *"Next time bring a smaller bottle. You are lucky today. Agent Gerta is in a good mood and says you may take it with you."*

The unexpected security quibble has further scrambled my weary brain and now that I've settled into my window seat with two others to my left, I realize my contact solution was tossed back into my carry-on now stuffed inside the overhead bin. Merd! I hate to be the pain-in-the-ass window seat passenger, but wait I must since the jet is now taking off. My stomach is growling for food, but is a bit leery of what might be served. The beverage cart rolls up and I'm trapped

---

33

for sure. The couple next to me is conversing in Italian. I am invisible to them. The Italian beauty is finishing her smoked almonds. Here's my shot. I tap her arm and point to the overhead (kudos to the passenger across the aisle who pantomimes my intentions). My faith is restored in human kindness as her boyfriend offers to heft my bag down for me. I dig out the contact solution and am so giddy, I forget to use the facilities while I'm already up. Ugh. As I convince myself to hold it until things become more urgent, my eyes begin to burn with that stinging sensation that comes from lack of sleep. The reflection in my personal video monitor displays purple and puffed circles forming under my eyes. But alas, steaming hot towels are being passed around again. Guess I'll wait to see what meal is allotted before passing out. KLM got it right with veggie pasta, couscous with asparagus, red pepper, radicchio and a surprisingly moist and delicious apple cake for dessert.

Naptime results in a few decent hours of shut eye, but I wake to aching shoulder pain and a violent urge to pee. I picture myself springing into a grand jete across the Italians, when two minutes into my fantasy the lovely *Maria* (yes, I named her) unbuckles her seatbelt (good sign) and begins to put on her shoes. As I exit the row, my enthusiasm and recent acrobatic fantasy cause me to land somewhat awkwardly smack onto another passenger's foot across the aisle. My apologetic gaze meets her *"You Clumsy American"* glare. It's a relief when returning to my seat to see her eyes shut and back asleep.

The attendants are handing out something, a fun and refreshing strawberry sorbet snack. Just to be safe, I take *Align*, a digestive pill. Airline food is not to be trusted. Hey, are we there yet? What time is it?

ARRIVAL

Two hours later we land safely in Kilimanjaro and everyone applauds. After filing off the plane, all passengers haphazardly queue up for Customs and Immigration. I spot an empty *"Nothing to Declare"* line. While a nice couple guards my carry-on luggage, I walk over to inquire about this *special* line. As I approach the official looking man, he shakes his head *"No Way"* and points me back to the cattle line. And why is everyone holding a blue card except me? On the flight I noticed the Italians each had one clipped to their tray tables after returning from the lavatory, but my seat held none. I figured it was because of my ingenious online registry with the Tanzanian Embassy weeks before departure. *"Excuse me. Is everyone required to fill out these blue cards?"* Fellow herd mate nods *"Yes."* I try to remain calm as my position shifts forward to third in line closer to the immigration officer. Quickly I hustle over to a stack of blue cards, then back to claim my spot. I give it my best grammar school legible handwriting, repeating in my head, *"Don't screw up, don't screw up."* Finished and sweating, but I'm NEXT!! A beautiful official stamp smacks onto my passport and I am wished a happy journey.

I stagger into the baggage claim area with trepidation, but am feeling too drowsy to worry .... yet. The luggage carousel snakes around very slowly. With each rotation a new assortment of luggage appears, except for mine along with a few others with worried ponems (Yiddish for face). Another two hours pass, ok maybe only twenty minutes, and still no navy duffel bag o' mine appears. My inner voice warns, *"Do NOT cry or bite your lip."* Could the Epic guides meeting us have fetched it already? Surely, that must be it. With hope in my heart, I scan the crowd for a sign imprinted *"FREEMAN."* But there is no such rescue in sight. Another forty minutes drag on and the luggage belt sadly stops. *"Are there any more bags left to unload?"* I look behind the magic curtain with great hopes of spotting my bag. Fellow Brit passenger, whom I later come to know as Martin, answers my anxious gaze with his.

—

"That's it, I'm afraid. Ours didn't make it either." I look back to check the adjacent belt one more time. *"Wait, could that be my navy duffel?"* IT IS! Oh thank you baggage gods! My fatigue is magically lifted, and I whiz through customs without questions asked or searching probes (I surely look quite pitiful by this point).

Outside the customs area are various tour company reps holding up passenger name plaques. And there it is at last, *EPIC TOURS FREEMAN*. I am greeted enthusiastically with *"Jambo"* (hello in Swahili). Our group's physician, Rob Barbour, introduces himself as well as our van driver, Ake. I am also introduced to Michael, a friend of Neil's, who had coincidentally just arrived on the same KLM flight. It's an hour's drive to accommodations at *The Arusha Coffee Lodge*. On the way, we get to know a little more about Dr. Rob. He charmingly explains how he's raising his two kids, four and seven years old, as monkeys. He's adorable with a cute as hell accent, the sort any woman wouldn't mind his looking after her if any illness befell her on this or any adventure. Michael and I try to muster polite conversation, but we are both too delirious with fatigue. Arrival at the lodge is a grateful relief and looks warm and inviting. The plantation is set smack in the middle of Tanzania's largest coffee plantation surrounded by acres of berry laden coffee bushes. Upon arrival we are greeted with divine, creamy iced coffee beverages, and then escorted to individual lodges. The rooms are equipped with a loveseat, coffeepot, mini-fridge, and a picturesque mosquito netted king bed. Fantastic! Unfortunately, my cell phone still doesn't work. Suddenly I feel homesick, so out of contact with my family. I begin to run water for a long awaited bath and the phone rings! It's Mac and just the sound of his voice gets my own water works going. After our chat, I bathe, take an *Ambien*, climb inside the mosquito netted bed, and at long last, pass out horizontally.

Waking relaxed and fresh, I am so glad to have opted for a travel rest day in Arusha. After breakfast, Michael and I decide to check out the nearby *Arusha Cultural Center*. We don't expect much from its shabby street appearance, but are delightfully surprised at the variety and abundance of African trinkets and artisan pieces for sale. It is actually a cluster of four different shops. Upon leaving, we notice construction of a *"New and Improved"* complex on the adjacent property, soon to house all of the stores we just visited.

Upon return to the lodge we meet the rest of our group, freshly delivered via private jet. After Neil and I embrace in a big hug and kiss, he introduces the rest of the party. I will begin with Emily, since she instigated this adventure. She and Neil became friends via her husband (owner of the private jet) and bonded further adventuring on an African safari taken two years prior. I form an instant girl crush (sounds better than envy) on this tall, slender, beautiful thirty year young woman of Asian heritage. Next is Eric, friend and work associate of Emily's, also in his thirty's. He strikes me as the perfect double for Keith Richards of *The Rolling Stones*. He has a wiry build with high energy and an easy grin. The third female in our group is also an invitee of Emily's, her longtime friend and mentor from college days at Wellesley. She greets me warmly. I like her immediately for her smile and the fact that she's closest to me in stature and in age. I admire her close cropped hairstyle and secretly regret not chopping mine off before the expedition. Dr. Rob introduces us all to Joseph, our "head guide," who has reportedly climbed the mountain no less than 150 times.

We amble through the coffee lodge courtyard to an al fresco lunch and a Kili briefing. The six of us express our mutual fears and expectations with Dr. Rob:
What is the success rate of hikers reaching the summit?
What altitude sickness symptoms might we expect?
Is malaria a cause of concern? Will we see much wildlife?
How many hours will we climb each day?
What should we wear and expect tomorrow, our first day?

Joseph takes our pulse rates and notes blood oxygen levels with a finger monitor that he will use later for comparisons as the altitude increases. Dr. Rob stresses the importance of hydration and its by-product of *"clear and copious pee,"* taking it slow and easy on the climb, and letting him know of the slightest of problems before they potentially become bigger.

After lunch, Neil and I fiddle with my cell phone and try to figure out why it isn't working as it should. We are not successful, so he loans me his Blackberry to call home. When I reach Mac, he intends to check with AT & T to find out why my phone is not getting coverage. We return to our lodges to organize for the morning departure. Uh oh, I have been mosquito bitten. I sure hope that skeeter was full of caffeine from the coffee orchard and not malaria!

When our group meets for dinner, the menu is fabulous and the food is as delicious as it sounds on paper. By dessert, I am too full to order the yummy sounding pistachio covered cardamom custard. I vow to eat dessert first when we return from the climb. However, the long and lean Emily does order dessert. I am convinced that she has a wooden leg. Damn her, I mean, bless her heart!

After desserts are served, Epic Private Journey's Director Brad Horn arrives. He is a trifecta combination of Australian born actor Hugh Jackman, TV's *Dr. McDreamy* of *Grey's Anatomy*, and *Survivor* show host, Jeff Probst. I try not to ogle. As if his presence isn't unnerving enough, alongside him stands a poster boy for outdoor adventure, Kevin. He looks to be in his early thirty's, six-foot-two all-American and perfectly adorable. You know the Disney twinkly eyed sort? Kevin hails from San Diego and is soon to be Brad's western sidekick for Epic Expeditions. Obviously, there will be no shortage of eye candy on this expedition, for us gals at least.

—

THE HIKE UP

Despite my requested 6 a.m. wake up call, I am awakened instead at 5 a.m. by what sounds to be a Muslim prayer call. It's quite beautiful and exotic to my ears. I silently pray they heed their words of peace and love. The next sound or squawk seems to be coming from a nearby monkey. *Cheetah, is that you?* I lie awake in the comfy netted bed telling myself, *"Go on, get up .... you know you can't sleep anymore now. Get a head start, make some tea, and stretch out with a few sun salutations."* I do what I'm told. I get out of bed and immediately spray down with *Deet* repellent. Hey, I'm not taking anymore chances! As I pull on my hiking boots I notice one crew sock missing, but shortly the mystery is solved. This could very well forebode my hiking ineptitude. I am wearing three socks on one foot.

After breakfast and a *Cheerio* to Cheetah who we spot prancing about the lodge's rooftop ledge, we climb into Epic's jeep transports. The ride to *Machame Gate* provides a kaleidoscope of colors and emotions for me. We pass scenic golden fields of corn and sunflowers dotted with goats and cows. The colorful locals sport assorted sized baskets balanced atop their heads while chatting on cell phones.... an oxymoron, right?! We are told this is a relatively new convenience for residents who just a few short years ago didn't even have access to landlines. Speaking of phones, Neil received a text message from Mac saying AT&T has switched my cell to international, so it should work now. That's great, except I left it back at the lodge since it wasn't working. Well then, text charges will be one expense I won't have to worry about.

We are directed to look to our left. There she rises in her full glory, Mt. Kilimanjaro. In my head Toto begins to sing, *"As sure as Kilimanjaro rises like Olympus above the Serengeti I seek to cure what's deep inside, frightened of this thing that I've become."* Hey Toto, I'm just frightened of THIS THING OVER THERE!!

43

When we arrive at *Machame Gate*, there looks to be around fifty or so other hikers milling about. To our astonishment and frank embarrassment, we learn that our intimate group of six will have forty-five porters along with six experienced guides plus Epic Crew members Dr. Rob, Brad, and Joseph to accompany us! Some will be assisting us on the climb, others will be hauling tents, sleeping bags, cooking essentials, and bathroom gear. Before we get started on our first day's hike, we make bathroom stops and top off our bottles and camelbacks with fresh water. Assistant Guide Sam, easy to spot with his brightly colored red head wrap, is introduced as our hike leader. We are given strict specific instructions NOT to get ahead of him (as if) or we'd receive swift admonition, *"Behind ME!"* We proceed to hike eleven miles through a lush tropical rain forest for six hours, from 5,906 feet elevation to first camp's elevation of 9,777 feet. To prevent altitude sickness we hydrate as often as possible and per Dr. Rob's recommendation, we begin taking half a tablet of *Diamox* twice a day. The wiry porters astound us as they pass by, carrying various degrees of heavy equipment, many balancing atop their heads, so strong, agile and graceful. We notice several are actually wearing quite flimsy worn sneakers. A member of our group brought along Swedish gummy fish for a sugar smacking energy charge and they're an instant hit with us all, crew members included. We're like a group of kids holding out our hands, *"More please?"*

The morning walk is quite pleasant, and I am greatly relieved there are no swarms of mosquitoes. As we walk along, Brad and Dr. Rob begin their *Great Gaiter Debate.* Apparently, it's been an ongoing subject of contention between the two of them for a number of years, the friendship going back to school rugby days.

Brad to Dr. Rob, *"Why don't you wear gaiters, man?*

Dr. Rob defends, *"I really don't feel the need to bother with* them. Watch, he'll wear them everyday until the last day when it's the muddiest of all. I think he wears them just for the look."

Brad shaking his head, "Man, they save my pants and shoes from getting dirty."

Dr. Rob laughs, "But you're wearing shorts!"

Brad turns to the group, "Well you guys should give them a go and see which one of us is right."

I chose not to wear gaiters today, but after a quick scan of my dirt caked pant's leg, I wish I had.

At last, we break for lunch. Right off the path is a picnic table complete with cheese, bread, soup and fruit, but I'm still so full from breakfast that I can't and don't eat much (BIG mistake). The load off my feet feels a*ahh* so good. However, we don't linger here and continue hiking until we reach the edge of the forest at dusk. Porters who had walked on ahead greet us at camp enthusiastically. They are joined together in a circle, clapping, singing and dancing. Emily and I join in, captivated by the energetic rhythm and beat. Hold on .... I recognize a few words of their song. Can it be? YES! It's HAKUNA freakin' MATATA, not Disney's, but the original Swahili version. Who knew? This was most definitely the highlight of my day!

After this, there's not much time for orientation inside our tents, but we do the best we can. My clean up basically consists of a full body wipe down ala *"Fresh Bath Travel Wipes."* For my face I use *"Oil of Olay's Facial Age Defying Wipes"* that evidently aren't working for me. Here's the harsh truth. While hiking today, leader Sam is asked (by some fool) to guess our ages. He guesses "fifty-six" for me. I just celebrated my fifty-fifth birthday. It's a little painful to hear, but what could I expect really .... in broad day lit jungle of

---

45

Africa, exposing my face au naturelle, stripped of age-fighting make-up, line reducers, firmers, concealers, re-vitalizers, fillers, light adjusters, and smoothers?!

At camp, there's a short seminar on portables usage, referred to as "*squat potties.*" They are appropriately nick-named, squat to the ground and bear a striking resemblance to a toddler's training potty, only a tad bit larger. There's a pump on one side that fills the base with water, much like the head on a sailboat. We are directed to pump until a proper amount of water fills the bowl and when finished, we are to pull out a handle at the base that allows "stuff" to empty into a hidden basin. The next morning a porter removes the under bowl and dumps out the waste. A roll of toilet tissue is supplied, but after my first experience, I remind myself to also bring along sanitizing hand wipes. I find myself appreciative for dedicated attendance in Pilates and yoga classes, as the squat potty requires unexpected thigh strength.

As the temperature begins to drop, I change into fleece pants and switch from nasty, sweaty boots into comfy crocs (which are delightfully fleece-lined). We are called to the circular mess tent for dinner and by the time I find my seat, I begin to feel dizzy and queasy. The room is spinning. I feel hot and clammy and fear what may come next. I lower my head down between my knees and pray that I don't puke during the first course, ruining everyone's dinner. Dr. Rob instructs me to lie down on the tent floor and place my feet upon the seat of my folding chair. Dinner is served. Food is the last thing I desire at this moment, but the doctor strongly encourages me to eat. I bite into a piece of bread, but it's like trying to chew a thick and absorbent paper towel. I can barely swallow. Hot tea and clear leek broth are offered. I force my-self to drink both, understanding the importance of hydration. I begin to feel a little better, but not quite normal. I am also feeling embarrassed and ashamed. Joseph takes everyone's pulse and oxygen saturation rates again. To my relief, mine checks out okay. Rob theorizes that my body is freaking out

---

given the weird combination of jet lag, time and altitude changes. My personal diagnosis is low blood sugar, knowing there's no way I could have consumed enough calories to match expended ones today on our lengthy hike.

Neil asks our guides to go over the next day's plan. What time are we to wake, what to wear, what time are we departing, where are we going, and what kind of terrain could we expect? After all points are covered, we return to our orange and khaki tents in a dark mist and bed down. I don't think a three inch foam mattress has ever felt so heavenly. However from 8 p.m. to 6 a.m. sleep is fitful, mostly due to the fact my bladder fills six times during the night. Finding the toilet tent in total darkness proves to be quite a challenge. My worst fear is coming true. I feel like a blind eighty year old Alzheimer patient, tripping on nearby tent stakes with no bearings as to the exact location of the potty tent or the way back to my own tent. At one point, I simply stand and stare up at the incredibly beautiful starry filled night sky wonder-ring if I might wind up remaining outside the rest of the night. I am too tired to panic and find myself quite honestly amused at my predicament. A lighthouse comes to mind. I slowly make a 360 degree turn with headlamp in place and behold, there appears a glorious sight...... the potty tent!

My next challenge is finding the way back to our tent. As if losing the potty tent wasn't ridiculous enough, I come close to unzipping someone else's tent, but thankfully notice familiar backpacks sitting outside the flaps of our own tent. I giggle to myself and wonder if that tent inhabitant thought someone was attempting a midnight booty call? But poor Cousin Neil, I fear my zipping in and out of our tent for multiple potty runs is robbing him of a good night's rest. At least I am peeing, the seal of approval for proper hydration. Why am I such a camel during the day? Sure wish I could switch my bladder's timetable to daytime frequency.

Morning finally arrives, with welcome relief that last night's queasiness has disappeared. I am well awake way before the 6:30 a.m. *"Good Morning"* announcement. A staff member *knocks* at our tent offering a choice of tea or hot chocolate. Nice touch. At 7:00 a.m. breakfast is served in the mess tent of hot and delicious oatmeal, toast accompanied with choices of butter, honey, peanut butter, scrambled eggs, bacon, sausage and cereal.

After getting tents organized and personal belongings fully packed, we line up at 8 a.m. Today we hike five miles to *Shira Camp* at 12,598 feet elevation, a "short day's hike." What someone fails to mention is that after crossing a valley and a stream, we continue another four hours up a Holy Mother of G-d vertical, rocky, and steep incline that's seriously tough on the quads, especially for this short legged gal. I am determined to drink and eat plentiful today to prevent another ill afternoon. We climb through billowy clouds after a sunny morning where we are warm enough to peel off outer layers by 11:00 a.m. We are excited to have a clear view of Kili along the way as well as her "little sister" *Mt. Meru.* Even in this escalating altitude, large clusters of white, red, and pink impatiens dot the hills above and below us. The terrain has changed dramatically from yesterday's lush rain forest to heather, and then to drier moorland at the Plateau. Michael, aka *"Mr. Gadget,"* pulls out his altitude meter which shows us at 15,000 feet, the same level as Mt. Fuji. Now that is pretty friggin' awesome!!

One of our guides, Noah, has become my constant companion. He makes sure I walk *"pole, pole,"* which is Swahili for slow mo. All of the guides are fantastically attentive and supportive, caring for me as they would their mother or aunt. Noah points out the best foot and handholds along the rocky traverse upward. *"How are you doing Ms. Sue? Maji, Maji"* (pronounced Mahee), a Swahili reminder to **DRINK MORE WATER DAMMIT!**

At the end of the day I feel fatigued, yet accomplished, by the time our beautiful camp appears. This afternoon we are greeted yet again by our amazing porters' happy and energetic welcome song and dance, literally against the backdrop of Kili herself. The tall, slim, jester hat wearing chant leader is Hapsan. He leads the porters in their daily song and dance, which he divinely improvises and choreographs as the spirit moves him. I say divine because each performance is a flawless fusion of glorious and exuberant jubilation. *"Na Na Na Na, Na Na"* are the only words we recognize to join along in chorus, the rest is Swahili.

The winds have definitely picked up now and as the sun dips, so does the temperature. I am praying it is not another six potty pee-time night. I'm eager to get to the tent to wash the day's rocky dust from my face. Neil and I learn the crew has set up separate tents for us. I must admit, I look forward to the extra move about space inside the tent. And no doubt Neil will sleep better without my frequent tent zipping. The best part is the location of my tent, close to the potty tent and smack next to a huge rock. I'm sure I can't miss this middle of the night landmark. The bad news is that there is still no cell signal. I worry that Mac thinks I've dropped dead (and that he's already spending the insurance $$$).

Afternoon tea time is called. I don't want to ruin my appetite for dinner, so I snack lightly. Good thing I restrained myself as dinner is plentiful ... pumpkin soup, potatoes, string beans with carrots, cauliflower, fried chicken, and fresh pineapple for dessert. Outside the round dining tent it is windy and freezing, but the sky is clear with stars aglow. Inside my tent, I set out clothing layers for tomorrow's predicted cool start. Dr. Rob promises it will warm again by noontime. As I caterpillar into my bundled cocoon, a familiar lullaby is resonating from a neighboring tent. I am instantly soothed by its rhythmic bass sound. Someone is snoring exactly like my husband. Now shush, don't you dare tell Mac I described his snoring as soothing after all the times I've reached over the bed to punch him to make it stop, rather subdue. But then again, I wouldn't have to punch him if he slept in a tent ten feet away from me!

49

I sleep fairly well, except for suspecting my tent's inclined, er reclined, placement might very well cause me and my sleeping bag to slowly roll down to lawd-knows-wheres-ville. On the other hand, I have read about the respiratory benefits of sleeping with your head raised higher than your feet ... Sweet. Resting and breathing easier now (thanks to my head raise), I remember hearing that tomorrow will be a long haul, seven hour, 2,592 foot climb to *Lava Tower* followed by a descent into *Barranco Valley*, but not as strenuous as today's. I hope it's the truth.

BULL SHIT.... it turns out to be effing hard!! I should've made Dr. Rob pinky swear. The negative connotation of the expression *"Take a Hike"* is never so clear. Sure, the incline isn't very steep, but it is frigid cold with winds blowing from twenty to twenty-five knots. The two hour descent to camp for altitude acclimation is difficult for me. Fatigue is setting in and my eyes are burning from staring at footing to prevent an ass bustin'. My nose, albeit a far distance from my bum, is a major pain in the ass. It drips constantly throughout the day's hike and is a major nuisance. I can hardly take a drink for having to tether my nose. My mistake was bringing an extra kerchief treated with bug protection. Little did I know, it had not gotten softer with washing. To make matters worse, I have probably been sticking cancer causing chemicals up my nose all day. On a positive note, we came across a very cool sight today, *Lava Tower*. As its name implies, it's a very large tower of black beautiful volcanic rock.

But back to me ... tonight I plan to dig into my dirty clothes bag for the soiled, but soft bandanna, disgusting as that sounds. I am certain today officially marks the end of my reign as my older brother David's JAP (Jewish American Princess) sister. My proudest moment today was taking a poop behind a rock en route. However, I didn't pee as much, so am hoping that's not a bad omen for another all-niter. At camp I just want to crawl into my bed sack, skip dinner and go to sleep. I am that tuckered out. Inside the privacy of my tent, I brave checking my compact mirror for witchy-wiry chin hairs. EGADS, ugly doesn't begin to describe what I see! My eyes are glazed in roadmap pink with swollen lids, while the under eyes are perfect specimens for cosmetic ads featuring the "before." My nose, er, rather beak, is scaly and red. My hair is funky (in a bad way), matted, and gooky. Oh why didn't I bring a baseball cap for camouflage?! Meanwhile, Emily emerges from her tent looking like an REI model, gorgeous silky black hair, flawless Asian complexion, impeccably dressed and unruffled. She is quite literally walking, er hiking, perfection. I want to hate her, but I can't. She is so damn sweet and kind. I get over my miserable appearance, as if I have a choice, and concentrate on the utterly incredible scenery. We are halfway, and there stands majestic Kili as our camp's scenic backdrop.

Dinner begins with bruschetta followed by sweet potato soup, pasta with veggies, and for dessert is sweet watermelon. When questioned as to our hydration levels and peeing amounts, I confess to a less than plentiful flow on today's climb. Dr. Rob asks how many liters I consumed during the day and from my response of *"three,"* he bounds into a lecture on the importance of proper fluid amounts to maintain hydration. At the time, it really seemed like I was drinking a lot, but apparently it was not enough. He warns I must make up for it during the night by drinking an additional liter. Good Gravy. I might as well relocate my sleeping bag into the potty tent itself. To my relief (literally) during the course of dinner, I excuse myself twice to pee and again directly after dinner. The pee, she is clear, so my opinion is that I'm just not much of a day tinkler.

Another topic of conversation at dinner, beyond bodily functions, is Brad's announcement of award nominations. He asks us to submit one for each group member. His plan is to present them at an awards dinner banquet post climb, back at the lodge. How fun! When I return to my tent, I scribble

---

down award ideas quickly in case my brain collapses before my body does. Tonight there is little sleep, with four bathroom trip interruptions plus a major sinus headache. However, I am comforted by the oozing warmth of a body heat adhesive strip and hand warmers.

After a fairly decent night's rest, the camp starts rattling about by 6:00 a.m. Although wake-up isn't until 6:30 a.m., my bladder decides otherwise. So I reorganize, repack and stuff dirty, stanky clothes back into my duffel. We huddle into the chilly breakfast tent and begin to warm fingers inside our armpits ala Molly Shannon's character *Mary Katherine* in the movie "*Superstar*" so that Joseph can get accurate pulse readings and oxygen saturation levels. It doesn't hurt that our morning circulations get an unexpected jump start. We just about choke from laughter when prim and proper Jan remarks, *"Michael, I was craving your nuts at midnight!"* She was still kvelling over the delicious nut mix he'd shared with us at yesterday's tea-time.

After a hot breakfast, we make pit stops, place duffels outside tents, fill camelbaks, and queue up for the day's trail. Dr. Rob gives a quick lesson in nose blowing sans kerchief, just straight out into the air. Although it works great, it still requires usage of a bandanna, tissue, or in my case today, a gloved hand, to wipe lingering residual moisture. I am reminded of a Caribbean sailboat trip taken years ago with my parents, husband, brother and sister-in-law. One of the crew mates named Serge, a Frenchman, routinely wore a bandana tied around his neck and as the week progressed, my sister-in-law began to refer to it as his "snot rag." I don't know why I remember his name because typically I just about forget my own. During this climb I am gaining a more respectful perspective on Serge's "snot rag" and now wish to hell I had packed half a dozen more!!

Day four we start out in warm layers, but within an hour we peel them off again. We uphill boulder climb *Barranco Wall* for three hours to 13,780 feet. It's a blast, not unlike climbing a gym rock wall. Clouds begin to hover and we add back outer layers plus gloves. The descent to *Karanga Valley* provides gentle ups and downs over rocks with boulders dotted with ice and running streams. We arrive at "scree school" where we learn the "rest step," a safety maneuver that involves vertical footing over fine gravel. This is in preparation for the final summit which is covered in scree near its upper portion.

Before we continue the rest of today's hike, we all make bathroom stops. For us girls, that entails not only finding a large rock to squat behind, but also scoping out any possible voyeurs from above or below. Neil earns extra points for frequently expressing empathy over the female demise. Guys have it so easy with their exterior plumbing. As much as I feel blessed in experiencing the miracle of childbirth three times, it just doesn't seem fair how much Eve screwed us over. However, I am never so grateful for my yoga practice than on this climb, not just for increased flexibility and strength, but at this moment for *Malasana* pose. For those non-yogini's, this is a basic wide footed squat position with palms pressed together at the heart. You get the picture.

As we tarry on, it begins to rain and we pull out, put on our Gore-Tex jackets. Within five minutes, the rain changes to sleet and we see Kili's peak blanketed with fresh snow. What a beauty! There is more rock climbing, but it is not as strenuous as the previous day's. On a few downhill spots, we must use more caution due to recent icy additions. We pass my airport buddies (the ones with the delayed luggage), and we learn that one of them, Martin, is terribly ill with altitude sickness. Lucky for him, Dr. Rob is along and offers help by dosing him with medication to curb his loss of fluids. An hour later, we run into Martin again and he has sprung back to his spry ol' chap happy camper self.

We spy our tents in the distance at last. Neil estimates we'll make it in a mere thirty minutes, but distance is a wily wabbit on this mountain. In actuality, it takes us another

---

TWO hours climbing up, down and around, until we actually arrive at camp. The porters greet us yet again with song and dance, but today all I want to do is polka to the potty tent. We have lunch at 2 p.m. of vegetable soup, fries, and slaw. There is also cucumber salad and chicken. Dessert is an interesting combo of avocado and orange slices. Dr. Rob encourages all to drink at least 1.5 liters before dinner and sends us back to our tents to refresh. For me, that means washing hands, full body wet wiperizing, and a change of underwear and socks. The afternoon gives us much appreciated ample time to relax and unwind. The best news of the day is finally obtaining a network signal strong enough to call home. Again, it's sooo good to hear Mac's voice!

Tea time is announced, and I smell my all-time favorite snack - popcorn! I've taken the doctor's prescribed hydration, followed by the typical bodily reactions. Between the extra hydration and more food than I've ever consumed in my life at any given meal, there are no shortage of number two's either. I can't help but dread that cause and effect as we make the final climb to the summit.

The sun begins to set, as does the temperature. Following dinner, it's time to snuggle into tent bedding. This is no simple feat, but I have implemented a system. I insert the flannel pouched liner into the sleeping bag first and attempt to line up zipper to zipper with the main bag, then I shimmy down inside the liner section while grasping tight its upper edges and scooch back up until my head nestles against the hood section. Next, I place my headlight under the pillow for easy access for those middle of the night u-know-what's and lastly, I slip on the fleece gloves. I think the altitude is getting to me when I hear Mick Jagger belting out *"Gimme shelter, yeah, gimme shelter, yeah."* I start to yell, "DOES ANY-ONE ELSE HEAR THE STONES PLAYING OR AM I GOING ALTITUDE CRAZY?" Just then Neil shouts, *"Can you hear my Blackberry's lullaby?"*

54

At breakfast, Neil shares morning announcements gleaned from his Blackberry phone's news link. Actress Farrah Fawcett, who was documenting her cancer battle on *YouTube,* has died. But much more shocking news is the death of legendary pop star Michael Jackson, *"from an apparent heart attack."* Crass commentary abounds, *"was it some plastic surgery complication or AIDS from his pet monkey?"* I am shocked and sad he is gone from us, such a spectacularly gifted, but tormented artist.

Today is a half day hike to *Barafu Camp,* elevation of 15,092 feet, supposedly an "easy" trail, but alas, 'twas NOT SO EASY. We pass fascinating black towers of stacked lava shards. Brad explains this Ice Age formation was caused by briskly flowing lava that froze super quickly along its path. My buddy Noah encourages me to drink at every opportunity. He teaches me the expression *"Chami, Chami,"* which translates to "Happy, Happy." When I ask the language source, I cannot understand due to his thick accent. Most of the porters and guides come from the Maasai tribe, except for Noah and a few others. Most of the porters speak Swahili and encourage us to mimic their lyrical sayings.

As we hike, Neil shares humorous excerpts from the movie "The Hangover." We are beginning to suspect he may be getting a kickback for his frequent promos. I enjoy an easy exchange with Dr. Rob about our families. He tells me about his Camp Kigelia in Ruaha National Park, as well as their month long program for college art students. Oh, how I wish we had the funds to send daughter Kate, our arts major. I will suggest she add this to her own bucket list.

I endeavor to drink in the ever-changing scenery, but either my feet or balance won't and don't cooperate. EACH time I dare glance around, I trip! Jan and Emily walk together in stride, catching up on Wesley joint projects. Brad and Kevin brain-storm details for an American version of Epic Expeditions that Kevin will soon oversee. Emily and Eric discuss art topics, staffing, and upcoming gallery projects.

—

Kevin and Neil, both avid snow skiers, compare myriads of slopes they've each experienced. Mostly I amble along within earshot of Neil and Michael as they discuss latest gossip, marriages, divorces, cosmetic surgeries, bankruptcies, recoveries, fund-raisers, and various travel experiences. The most entertaining is Neil's enthusiastic touting of the Japanese engineered *Toto Washlet 5400* toilet, complete with automated lid, front and rear washer, warm air dryer and more. Conversations mostly graze my brain blurring into white noise, other times their discussions evolve into an audio book soundtrack. I cannot help but feel like a flea among this impressive group of climbers. Basically, my only common ground with this group is the climb itself and the color of our pee. I'm a simple homemaker and mom for G- sake. Excitement for me is typically the Sunday paper's bonus coupon clipper section!

We arrive at Barafu Camp (elevation 15,092 feet) by noon, so there's time to relax before lunch. This is the rest stop before our arduous midnight Summit departure. I try to sort clothing layers and configure some order for the afternoon's Summit wardrobe inspection. Sam is assigned to my tent as gear inspector. We discuss layer options and decide that given my heater adhesive pads, the outer Gore-Tex jacket can remain stashed in my backpack for later use if needed for wet conditions. Here I was complaining about my chronic runny nose when poor Jan seems to be coming down with a fresh cold right before the toughest part of our climb. Hopefully Dr. Rob can work his magic to help her feel better before Summit mobilization at 11:30 tonight, or rather 23:30. Naps are on order for this afternoon, but we are all leery of the prospect. We are told the climb will take eight hours to *Stella Point,* all in the dark with the aid of head spotlights, and then another two hours to *Uhuru* (the Summit) supposedly by sunrise. I am trying really hard to be Zen calm to control anxiety. *"It is what it is,"* or whatever it will be.

56

Lunch is soup, pasta and more veggies, which I skip to prevent Summit rocky number two's. I permit myself to wallow in formerly taboo white bread slathered in real butter. OH MY GAWD, it's pure heaven! How long has it been, nearly forty-five years?! Our guides offer their best summit advice: plentiful water consumption and to keep extra bottles wrapped in insulating cloth inside our backpacks to prevent freezing (cringe), place snacks in easy pocket reach, keep sunscreen on hand for the return descent in full sun as well as protective sunhats (due to near proximity to the equator), wear eyeglasses instead of contacts, insert new batteries into headlamps, lube liberally the interior and exterior of our nostrils, and keep the tube within reach for re-application. I am picturing snotcicles attached to my nose and face. Sure wish he had also recommended extra lube application to the upper lip area. For a week after the climb, mine molted like a duck on a hot summer's day. After hearing Brad's recount of a female climber whose frozen ponytail broke off at the summit, I am comforted by my relatively short hairstyle. We are also reminded to blow back into our camelbak tubes after each sip of water to avoid icy build ups. After describing my shortness of breath with this practice, I am told to blow into the tube without first inhaling too large a breath. The blowing technique is suddenly clear to me, *"Like blowing a shofar or conk shell."* Neil quips, *"O Sue, don't tell everyone you blew the chauffeur!"* My head spins around and my eyes bulge. By my shocked reaction, it's apparent I've never heard the joke so Neil enlightens me:

> *What was the gentile's response upon hearing the Jewish Holy Day custom of shofar blowing?*

> *You people sure are good to your help!*

~~~~~~

—

KILIMANJARO NATIONAL PARK
MACHAME GATE
ALTITUDE 1800M. AMSL

	E.T.A.
MACHAME GATE-MACHAME HUT	4.5 HRS
MACHAME HUT-SHIRA CAVE	3.5 HRS
SHIRA CAVE-SHIRA HUT	30 MIN.
SHIRA HUT-LAVA TOWER	3 HRS
LAVA TOWER ARROW GLACIER	1.5 HRS
ARROW GLACIER-SUMMIT	5 HRS
SHIRA CAVE-BARRANCO	6 HRS
BARRANCO-KARANGA	3 HRS
KARANGA-BARAFU	3 HRS
BARAFU-SUMMIT	6 HRS

Kilimanjaro National Park

First Day Picnic

Camp Welcome Song & Dance

Camp Site

Sleepwear

Squat Potty

Lava Tower

Barranco Wall

Guy's EZ Breezy Pit Stop

ENDLESS SUMMIT NIGHT

Our afternoon naptime from 5 p.m. to 10:30 p.m. amounts to some rest, but unfortunately no real sleep. Since resting in most of my layers, I now have only to add shoes, heater adhesives, down jacket, and warmer inserts into the $150.00 mitt gloves. And cue the "*Rocky*" theme song. At 11:00 p.m. we are called to queue up. I am ready at attention, front and center! Well, I thought so until Dr. Rob looks me over, up and down, "*Sue, where is your Gore-Tex jacket?*" With confidence I respond, "*In my backpack, as Sam instructed.*" He orders, "*Get it out and put it on. You'll need it!*" Brad is anxiously checking his watch, "*Queue up everyone. Time to head out!*" Meanwhile, I am awkwardly removing my backpack to fetch my Gore-Tex jacket, put it on, and then strap back on my pack. Brad's begins to freak on me, "*HURRY UP Sue!!*" Ay Caramba! Any manipulation of my hands requires the removal and re-fitting the *Super Alpine* mitts. I am ordered to queue up directly behind leader Sam, whom I adore. He has the Maasai demeanor, but quieter than most with a shy, dimpled grin.

And we're off! Unfortunately, within thirty minutes I realize these fancy schmancy mitts aren't working for me whatsoever. Yes, my hands are indeed quite warm, but they are also impeding my grasp on the hiking poles. Imagine trying to play golf wearing bulky oven mitts. Lesson learned – practice with ALL equipment! Note to self: *Upload mitts on eBay upon return home.* Not only am I having problems with the damn mitts, but I am beginning to overheat, the last thing I expected to happen on this hike. Even in sweaty yoga classes, I am typically the only student in downward facing dog covered in goose bumps. It's the middle of a dark, moon-less night. We're all wearing headlamps. I feel awkward and out of sync, plus my vision is impaired because my glasses are beginning to fog up. To make matters worse, the Gore-Tex pants are restricting my normal flexibility over each rock boulder. Two days ago I was picturing myself featured on the box cover of *Wheaties*, but at this moment I feel more suited to

---

cover for the Quaker Oats dude. It's sucky enough my legs are three inches shorter than the rest of the group's. Brad shouts from the rear *"Step it up guys....DON'T STOP MOVING!!"* I am not a happy hiker at this point. In fact, I'm close to tears. There are at least eight or more hours to go, and I feel like a miserable failure straight out the shoot, holding everyone up. Brad shouts again, *"HURRY UP GUYS!"* I want to turn around and slap the living daylights (ok, the living shit) out of him. Suddenly, his image morphs into a sinister whip cracking mush driver while we are transformed into his sled dogs. My inner mutt is whelping for relief from the pricey, suffocating, obtrusive mitts. I yell (inside my head), **THE HELL WITH BRAD!** What can he do, shoot me?! *"Sam,"* I whisper. *"I need to remove my jacket. I'm much too hot."* And oh sweet, sweet smiling Sam gently helps remove my jacket. I toss off the damn gloves and feel liberated despite the freezing temps. I can feel Brad fuming from the rear, but I am not giving up so easily.

Dr. Rob reminds us, *"Keep drinking guys and remember to blow back into the mouth piece."* We hike ever up and up. The stars are spectacular, but I cannot fully appreciate nor take the time to admire them for having to keep my lit head down watching each careful step. When it's time for a pit stop, the men are finished in a jiff as usual. Meanwhile we girls not only have to find a covert squat rock spot, when we are finished we still have four tight layers to pull back up and realign with crotch and hips. No easy task. By the end of these 24 hours, I don't even bother to check who might be peeping my pee spot because I am too tired to give a fig. Brad shouts impatiently, *"Hurry girls!"* I'm trying to conjure up Buddha and Moira, my beloved yoga instructor, *"Love All. All is well."* Neil hikes up to me, *"Sue, are you okay?"* I am hesitant to respond, afraid of saying something I shouldn't. *"Working on it, am just a bit annoyed right now; will explain later."*

Somewhere between 2 and 3 a.m., Brad is exasperated with our slower pace and pit stop delays. He suggests

—

66

dividing the group into two. I hate the idea of being separated from Neil. On the other hand, Brad will be off my back. The guys blast off while the girls remain with Sam, Noah, and Dr. Rob. Within seconds Dr. Rob is shouting words of encouragement, *"Good going Girls. Nice pace!"* I relax now, sigh with relief, and feel enormous gratitude for Dr. Rob's presence and for his reassurance. This is going to happen after all. We are accompanied by shooting stars and Venus on the horizon, but the only moons we might see tonight are our own.

At one memorable pee stop, I find what seems to be the perfect squat rock. As I head back to the path, Jan stops me.

Jan: *Sue, there is something stuck to your back.*

Sue: *Oh really, is it part of a bush or what?!*

Jan: *No, it's some kind of paper."*

Sue: *Wonderful. Leave it to me to trek all the way to Kilimanjaro and wind up with tissue stuck to my heel!*

Jan: *Ummm, no…. it looks like a Kotex pad.*

Sue: (horror struck) *Oh GROSS and YUCK, you're messin' with me, right?!*

Unfortunately, she wasn't. I can't believe any woman with the ability and guts to climb Mt. Kilimanjaro would be so unconscionable or disrespectful that she would toss a Kotex pad, used or unused, on this trail …. that is, unless she was unconscious, THEN it would be forgivable.

After this pit stop, we continue climbing, climbing for hours on end in a dull dizzy daze. There is no concept of time. Noah persistently reminds me to *"Drink, drink, Sue."* He tells me about his education and plans for becoming a licensed Kilimanjaro guide leader. We talk about his family and his desire for economic independence. He asks about my family too. The night blurs into a hint of sunrise shyly rising from below. Dr. Rob says reassuringly, *"Soon it will be light and we can turn off our headlamps."* But sunrise is in slow-mo and the darkness lingers much longer than anticipated. Africa's sense of time seems much akin to my husband's own unique time perspective. *"In a few minutes"* equates to around thirty to sixty minutes. *"Very soon"* is really one or two hours, and here in Africa *"just a short distance"* means at least an hour's walk. Dawn is approaching, and a strange sight appears off in the distance. I point in its direction.

> Me: *"Dr. Rob, what is that dome looking structure way over there? Is it a house, a scientific tent, what?"*
>
> Dr. Rob: *"Where, What?"*
>
> Me, pointing: *"See that dome looking thing?"*
>
> Dr. Rob: *"Sue, there's nothing over there, but snow covered rock."*
>
> Me, laughing: *"O yeah, I don't have my eyes in so I often see things that don't really exist."*

The pink sunrise is incredibly beautiful, but the glaciers facing us across the clouds are a breathtaking, mesmerizing sight. We still have several hours to hike before reaching the summit, and my heart sinks a little knowing our guides intended us to *".... catch the sunrise from the Roof of Africa"* as stated in their brochure. Finally we make it to *Stella Point*, but I secretly wish it is the final summit instead. It feels good to stretch out like a cat in the sun and use the "facilities." It saddens us to see the trash, even cigarette butts, left there. We eat snack bars brought from home and enjoy juice boxes

---

supplied by Epic, apply sunscreen and more lip balm before our final ascent.

Now we put into action our scree practice. Rob keeps pace behind us, keeping a watchful eye on our footing and gently corrects our technique when needed. The scree move is much like ice skating, or at least in my fantasy footing. This GRITS (girl raised in the South) hasn't had much experience in that arena either. And it goes like this: shift left foot forward slightly turned out, brushing against the earth while simultaneously lifting back right foot. As left foot hits ground, lock the knee and swing right foot forward. Repeat the same move with opposite feet and legs. The repetitive move is comforting to me and a distraction from the long distance ever upward in what seems at times to be more sand than gravel. Dr. Rob points, *"Almost there!"* Now we're on a snakelike path which I learn are called "switchbacks." We approach the summit's official *Uhuru Peak* at 9:45 a.m. and read the pinnacle's signpost:

"CONGRATULATIONS!
You are now at UHURU PEAK TANZANIA
Africa's Highest Point 19,344 feet
World's Highest Free Standing Mountain."

To be honest, I'm almost more exhausted than enthused about it. Emily and Jan embrace in a touching, tearful, emotional hug. I miss Neil like crazy now, wishing we could have shared this climatic moment together. There are handshakes and high fives all around. Our stoic Sam becomes surprisingly animated and asks if I will take a photo of him wearing my son's Martian fleeced cap. With great honor, I oblige him. We take group and individual pictures of our mutual success in actually making it to the tiptop. I choose yoga's *Warrior Pose* for my photo op. After all, to get to this *point* has been quite a battle of will and stamina. I pose victorious, wearing my son's florescent green fleece cap with attached flexible spiral-shaped antenna. Unfortunately, the photographer doesn't grasp my symbolic stance, so the actual photo depicts me not-so-much warrior-like as much as "Crazy Martian Lady" at Summit.

Crazy Martian Lady at Summit

Kili Sunrise

Glacier View

THE HIKE DOWN

At this moment, little did I know that getting down from this mountain would provide an even greater challenge. *"No time to dally,"* warns Dr. Rob. *"Let's make our way down now."* As we head down, my feet freeze (but not literally). Remembering a promise made to my nephew, I shout, *"My rocks, I promised to bring back lava rocks for my nephew!"* Dr. Rob and I quickly gather three rocks, toss them into my backpack, and downward we go. Hapsan is assigned to help me maneuver the intense and long downward scree slope. He grabs hold of my hand and I am euphoric. We are slipping, sliding, ever downward in finger lock grip, sometimes arm in arm. He grasps my arm tighter in steeper spots, saving me several times from skidding face downward the rest of the mountain. Occasionally, he lifts me completely off my feet. He's approximately six feet four inches tall next to little ol' five feet one inch me. Too bad that photo op was missed.

Our arrival at *Mweka Camp* clocks in shortly after 1 p.m. The boys are already in the mess tent eating lunch and looking beat, but pleased with their accomplishment. Neil and Eric practically flew down the mountain (both avid skiers), while Michael encountered mysterious symptoms of confusion, lethargy and dizziness on his return trek. He had been downing pack after pack of electrolyte gels, having great success with them on previous biking expeditions. Dr. Rob determines that Michael had consumed way too many, thus overloading his system. He also explains that alpine climbs do not produce as much body sweat as Michael's routine bike riding.

We are all exhausted, given we have been awake (which is questionable) and climbing either up or down since 11:15 the previous night. Math has never been my strong suit, but I think this adds up to about 14 hours solid! During lunch it is rumored the hiking distance for the afternoon may be cut shorter than originally planned. Alas, it turns out 'twas only a rumor indeed. The group is pleading for mercy that we might be given some much needed R & R time. Rob and Brad

—

confer, then return to us announcing a departure time of 2:15 p.m. for our night's final camp at *Mweka*. Moaning and groaning, we glance into each other's weary disappointed faces. Say it isn't true! We consider mutiny. Neil asks, *"Can't we hire a helicopter to pick us up?"* Brad and Dr. Rob muster up empathetic expressions and explain how we must make it to camp this night, otherwise the following day we'd have to hike another ten hours to the final gate. I am numb, except for my burning toes. Mostly what I hear is blah, blah, blah, no longer assuaged by their charming Australian accents. The harsh truth is now we girls have a mere forty-five minutes to recoup, freshen up the best we can, and change into lighter layers before another five an a half hour descent to *Mweka Camp*. Both big toes are super sore from the four hour vertical slam-jam into the tips of my boots. I dare not remove my boots for fear my feet will never fit back inside again. My brain cannot fathom how long it's been without rest nor can my legs. I try hard to figure it out, but in calculating the hours and what lies before us still, I feel like a deer caught in head-lights frozen in disbelief (or more like horror). I limp to my tent to repack and reorganize for our final camp. Back in the privacy of my tent and with a bountiful supply of tissue paper, I blow my nose and am struck by the combination of volcanic dust, snot, and blood grossosity that emerges. No one warned me of this nasty side effect. I am beyond fatigued, but grasp the importance of proceeding further downward today. I peel off layers of dirty socks, pants, shirts and stuff them into my ever growing lemon fresh plastic trash bag.

Here we go, five or more hours of hiking to final camp. My toes are no longer suffering in silence. They are screaming out with each painful rocky step downward, OUCH, OUCH, OUCHA. I have no choice, but to keep moving. The hiking poles help alleviate some of the weight. Sweet Noah offers to carry my pack, and I am ever so thankful for his assistance. Brad says if we speed up, we may be able to beat darkness. But we can't and we don't. Noah helps to strap on my head-

---

lamp, and we keep hiking down over what looks like a rocky dried creek bed. The headlamps seem to cast a magical spell over the rocky path. The rocks glow iridescent, *"Are those crystals?"* I ask. No one responds. I suppose they assume it's my crazy imaginary blind sighted world again. I'm thinking they're probably right. I begin to see an assortment of petrified monkey skulls, but I keep these visions to myself. The smooth part of the dirt path looks and feels underfoot as if wax coated, reminiscent of the miniature waxed candy bottles we used to buy as kids at the five and dime. Noah says, *"Soon rocky path becomes smooth road."* His remark energizes me, but shortly it dawns on me. Dang, it's another African distance teaser! I never do see or experience any smooth road, and there is no *"soon"* either.

We reach camp at 7:30 p.m. and upon arrival hear this announcement: *"Dinner ready in five minutes."* OK, first of all, I feel like crapola. I'm sweaty, nasty, kaput, and in need of a major wipe down that was going to require more than five minutes, followed by a change of clothing. Hungry is not on my list. HELL, I need five minutes just to remove my boots! And as I remove my boots and stinky socks, my toes are a woeful sight to behold. There are two swollen moon shaped blood blisters, one at the cuticle base of my right big toe and the other on my left foot's bossy toe. I shout over to Neil, *"I'm skipping dinner, am way more tired than hungry. When you see Dr. Rob, ask him to stop by my tent. I need toe advice."* And by the time I change into semi clean sleepwear, Dr. Rob appears. *"Let's take a look. OHH, this really needs to be lanced if you'll let me."* Knowing we had another long hike in the morning, I agree to the procedure. Luckily, I brought along a travel sewing kit, why I cannot say. Nonetheless the needle was coming in handy, although I had brought the wrong type mole skin for toe wrapping. Dr. Rob comes to the rescue again with some handy dandy bandaging wrap. The lancing doesn't hurt at all, and my toes actually feel more relieved.

Our final day's hike awaits us this morning as well as our porters who have gathered round for a grand finale performance…..the extended version. Dr. Rob translates their chanting for us, *"Don't take your pay to the pub or to the brothel, take it home to your wife and family!"* It was stellar! Brad collects group tips for the porters and suggests additional amounts for individuals who may have given us *"extra special assistance."* Before tips, their earnings amount to $8.00 a day. After their song and dance, I bestow Sam my fuzzy lime green Martian beanie, and he is oh so pleased! We also gather items to leave with them, our backpack rain covers, extra gloves, caps, batteries, wipes, and remaining energy bars. I begin to fantasize about getting back to a real bed and bath at *The Arusha Lodge.*

HELLZ YEAH FINAL DAY'S HIKE

Today we pretty much hang together as a group. The remaining hike runs through a tropical rainforest. It is indeed gently raining. Tall, green trees wrapped in vines climb up in reach for the sun. Ooey gooey mud oozes under our boots between each rocky step. Along the way, Brad sets in stride with me. He heard from Neil how much he upset me on summit night and wants to apologize. Over the course of the day, Neil and Michael separately report to me that Brad expressed sincere regret over it. To be honest, I'm glad to hear this, if only for the sake of his being more patient with the next petite menopausal hiker in a future group.

For the rest of our walk everyone has their share of missteps, slips and slides. Even the sure footed guides and porters lose their balance and land in the mud as do three others in our group. I confess to being most delighted when Brad's bum smacks down into the muddiest ditch of all, complete with a small flowing waterfall. ... Instant Karma?! We are a holy-moly, muddy, happy group at the finish. We sign our names, dates, and ages on a "proper" registration list in order to receive certificates of reaching the summit's peak. Locals hanging at *Mweka* hut offer to wash our boots for $2.00 a pair. There are also t-shirts for purchase. The one I choose says "**JUST DONE IT....Kili.**"

At our return transport, we celebrate with a delightful choice of Kili beer or champagne and delicious samosas, which are fried meat and veggie pies. We devour them with gusto (though my tummy pays for it later). We hoist ourselves up into the four-wheelers and ride back to the lodge with bellys full of beer, samosas, and weary triumph. We pass through a lovely agricultural village and see a familiar figure walking carefree alongside the road. It's Hapsan, my summit descent angel, easily identified by his tall, lanky body topped with his funky jester hat. We stop to wave and shout out a final "*Jambo!*"

We reminisce and compare personal highlights of the climb. Michael relates a disturbing conversation overheard on

—

81

his hobble down the mountain while flanked by Dr. Rob and one of the porters. The subject of AIDS arose and the porter began to question the doctor, revealing his lack of knowledge about the disease. *"My friends say if you take a shower after sex, you will not get AIDS."* That type of misinformation is why the AIDS virus is still rampant in Africa. Brad tells Neil that one of the guides from their safari two years ago recently died from AIDS. I did not realize how prevalent it remains in this part of Africa. The lack of educational awareness is shocking and so very sad.

Typical American fitness obsessed boomers are we, and our attentions divert back to us. We try to calculate calories burned through sheer exertion combined with the effect of altitude on our bodies as well. I am certain my caloric intake came no where near energy expended over the past five days, but without mirrors to check my butt view, I cannot evaluate shrinkage. Dr. Rob and Brad tell us that we will be amazed at our increased energy and lung capacity levels the week we return home due to the extreme altitude stress on our bodies. They predict a welcome home lung and heart fest!

Rainforest

Kili Beer

CELEBRATION

Returning to *The Arusha Lodge,* we are welcomed back with a tray of yummy iced coffees and then escorted back to our individual cottages. Praise Jeezus, a private room with indoor plumbing! I peel off my clothes and hardly recognize the body in the mirror. On my shoulder stands my mom shaking her head and pointing her finger at me, "S*tart eating NOW."* Ok Mom, I hear ya! There is no doubt my normal weight and curves will return within a few weeks. It's not as if I will continue climbing a 19,000 foot mountain. I promised myself a Waffle House visit upon my return and well, a promise is a promise!

The hot shower is pure nirvana, although the black coffee colored soap is a bit disturbing. I can't tell if the washrag is pulling off so much crud or if it's just the freaky colored soap. The toilet provides unexpected glee, no more squatting. It feels like ascending a royal throne (as if) and I laugh, realizing it's simply a standard height commode. Soon my Kili buds are knocking at the door, inviting me to join them for cocktails and I do. What else could I order but an Oh hell yeah, *Kilimanjaro Beer,* recovery beverage of champions. Someone in our group remarks, *"Well, now we can mark this one off our bucket list!"* I almost choke, "BUCKET LIST?! *This had not even been a remote blip on my radar!"* I am categorizing this as one of life's little surprise jokes.

We all assemble at dinner and clink our glasses in a celebratory toast, "To Kibo and to new friendships!" Dr. Rob points his finger at me, *"Sue, I wasn't sure you were going to make it, to be honest. I started to worry when you began seeing snow huts en route to the Summit. I was afraid you might be hallucinating until I caught what you said about not having your eyes in. Then it dawned on me you didn't have in your contacts."* I fess up, *"Well, good thing I didn't tell you about seeing monkey skulls on our final hike. Those weren't real, right?!"*

—

Brad presents our official certifications:

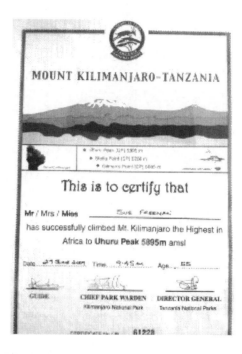

This is to certify that Sue Freeman has successfully climbed Mt. Kilimanjaro the Highest in Africa to Uhuru Peak 5895 amsl Date 27 June 2009   Time 9:45AM   Age 55
GUIDE CHIEF PARK WARDEN DIRECTOR GENERAL

Next he presents our individual awards:

ERIC: "Mountain Goat Award" for most likely to hike without poles, "Best Rocker Award" for his fashionable head bandana, and "Michael Jackson Award" for dancing at 18,000 feet to keep warm.

EMILY: "Jean Paul Gaultier Award for Alpine Fashion" for looking great on the mountain every day, and "Diamox Award" for consistency with urination.

NEIL: "Jay Leno Award" for keeping us laughing, "Best Promoter Award" for talking up the movie "Hangover" and

"CNN Award" for best connected. He wins a year's award at an IT Addicts Retreat.

MICHAEL: "Mad Hatter Award" for having caps for every scenario, "Nutty Gadget Award" for having all manner of gadgets, and "Jewish Santa Claus Award" for nightly treats at dinner.

JAN: "Best Dressed Ears on the Mountain Award" for wearing a pair of earrings that survived the round trip and the "She Said It Award" for the infamous line, "Michael, I was craving your nuts at midnight!"

SUE: "Mississippi Mountaineer Award" for being the most accomplished mountaineer in Mississippi and "Extra-Terrestrial Award" for the best effort to contact aliens with a silly hat on the summit.

BRAD: "Best Fall Award" for his graceful move on Day Seven into a mud wash, and "Best Jeff Probst Impersonation."

ROB: "Best Curly Eyelashes Award" for the obvious and "Incomplete Mountaineer Award" for lacking gaiters.

JOSEPH: "Best Pulse Taker"

KEVIN: "Best U.S. Outdoor Adventure Poster Child Award and "Scientology Award" for believing in things that clearly don't work. Michael is the runner up in this category.

HOME SWEET HOME

Most of the group departs the following morning via Emily's private jet. I depart late afternoon on a magic carpet ride. Well, it might as well have been. The thirty-two hours it takes to get home, including layovers in Amsterdam and Memphis, is a blurry piece of cake compared to climbing twenty-one hours straight.

My first morning back, I don't know how (probably still delirious), I decide to attend Pilate's class for a greatly needed stretch. There are hugs and a surprise gift from my yoga teacher. She presents a quote written on her calendar the exact date of my return, *"Most look up and admire the stars. A champion climbs a mountain and grabs one."* Suddenly my feelings of ineptitude are lifted. It took a lot of courage and determination to get up that mountain. Why shouldn't I be proud of this fifty-five year old piece of work? That night, I sink into my comfy bed with my heavenly pillow next to my sweet, ever snorin' husband and dream the guides are in the kitchen waiting for me to wake up. Training begins today for space travel! An even wilder dream…

Or is it?!

PERSONAL PICKS
AND
RECOMMENDATIONS

Zanbori 310 Skill GT Hiking Boot

Tip: Don't lace all the way up unless you want the feel of strangled ankles. Keep 2 top brackets unlaced and wrap laces back around to front, and then tie together.

Leki Yukon Aergon Anti-Shock Trekking Poles

Ergonomic handles, lightweight, & telescopic – saved my ass!

"Sombrero" sun hat

3 pairs lightly padded socks, 3 pairs heavy crew Smartwool

6 pair Ex-Officio bikini red panties

In case one gets lost, they can be used as flags.

3 long sleeve layering tops

2 pair long underwear, 1 silky, 1 thermal

REI Heavyweight MTS Bottoms felt yummy for sleeping & perfect for wandering outside for the potty tent.

3 pairs hiking pants, 2 khaki, 1 dark colored

Can fold to capri length. Outdoor Research Venture Pants ++.

Outdoor Research Women's WINDSTOPPER Gripper Glove

Outdoor Research Enigma Gore-Tex jacket

For cold and wet conditions.

Spare contacts

Lost one somewhere between Amsterdam and Arusha.

Travel towel & washrag

3 or 4 bandanas or handkerchiefs

For noses that tend to run like faucets.

Black Diamond Spot Headlamp, extra AAA's

For the G-d forsaken night potty runs + summit hike

Down jacket, Mountain Hardwear Nitrous Jacket

Rolls up tiny for packing and stuffing into backpack.

Camelback backpack & insulated tube

One with many pockets for extra bottles, snacks, lip balm.

Bakalava

Still makes my mouth water, though it's really a fleecy face & head cover and fun for masquerading as a ninja warrior.

Snack bars

Chocolates, energy bars & definitely, Swedish gummy fish.

—

Moleskin & scissors
Sanitary wipes
Large bathing wet cloths
Sewing kit
A needle might come in handy for lancing blisters.
Imodium
All of us dosed at one time or another for upset tummies.
Insect repellant
Only needed at the beginning of rainforest; mosquitoes are more of a problem on the Mississippi Gulf Coast.
Sunscreen for face
You will be next to the equator, and sunburns come easily.
Night facial moisturizer
Can't imagine how much worse my skin would have peeled without it.
Vaseline tube
For use on nose, lips, upper lip, especially on summit night.

**Can't Recommend

**Patagonia Storm Pants
They restrict flexibility necessary for climbing.
**Outdoor Research Alti Mitts
$$$$. Although they were warm enough, I couldn't hold on to the hiking poles and I wound up removing them altogether, *Ebay* bound.

SPECIAL MENTIONS

A mountain of gratitude to my Cousin Neil for the most exciting, unforgettable birthday present ever and for his love, friendship, and generosity!

Big kudos to *Epic Private Journeys* for great organization, best porters, top guides, good eats and for keeping us safe. **www.epicprivatejourneys.com**

Deep appreciation to Dr. Rob Barbour for protecting our health and well-being with vigilant care and concern: **www.afrikaafrikasafaris.com**

Funds are desperately needed to promote AIDS education & awareness in Tanzania. Where and how to donate: **www.amref.org**

In loving memory of *AmberJack*, 1996 - 2009

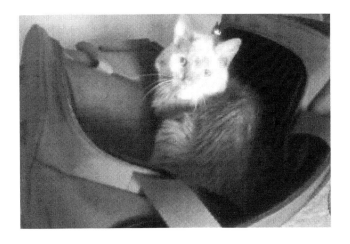

Made in the USA
Columbia, SC
01 May 2019